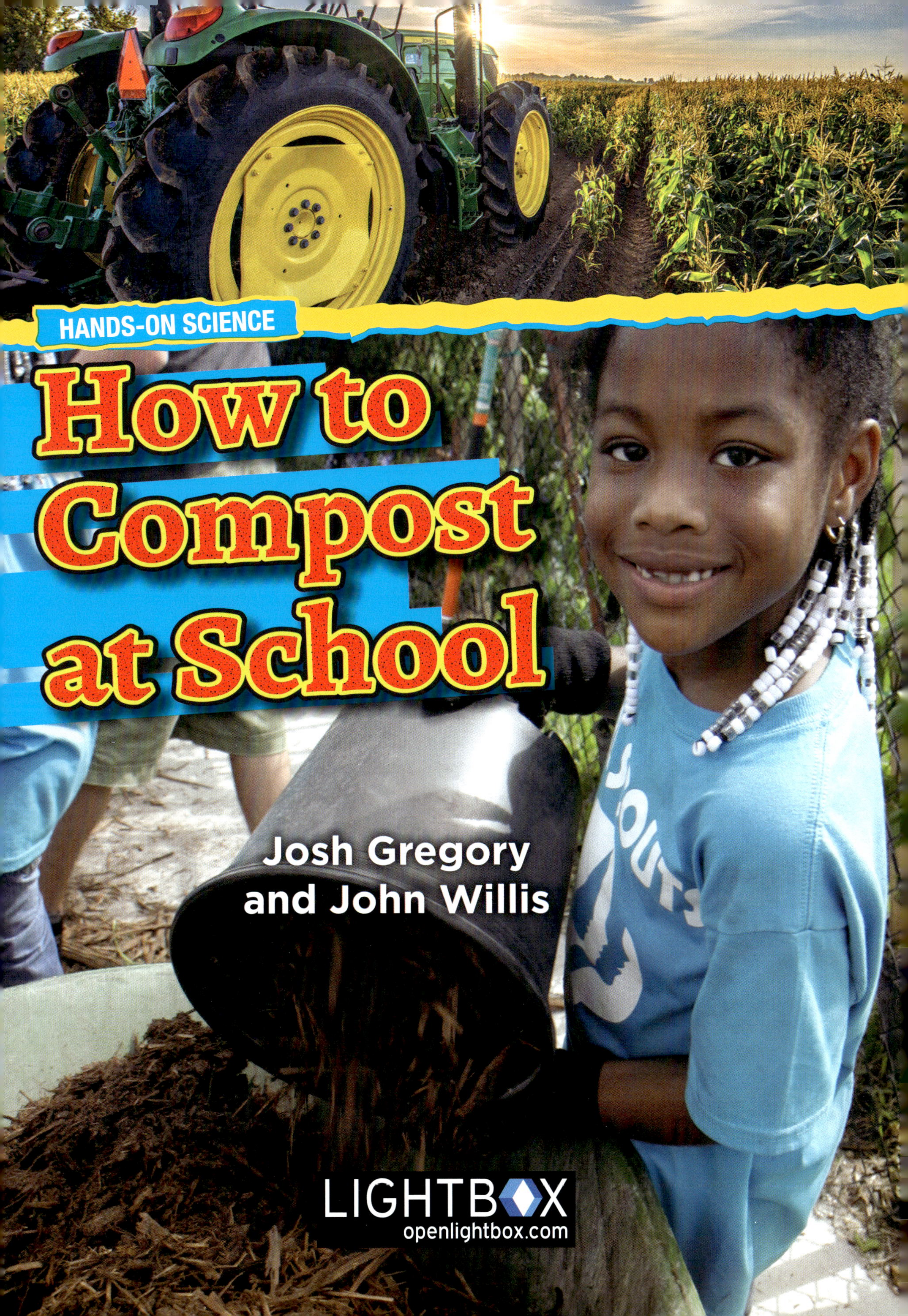
HANDS-ON SCIENCE
How to Compost at School
Josh Gregory
and John Willis
LIGHTBOX
openlightbox.com

LIGHTBOX

Go to **www.openlightbox.com** and enter this book's unique code.

ACCESS CODE

LBXF5569

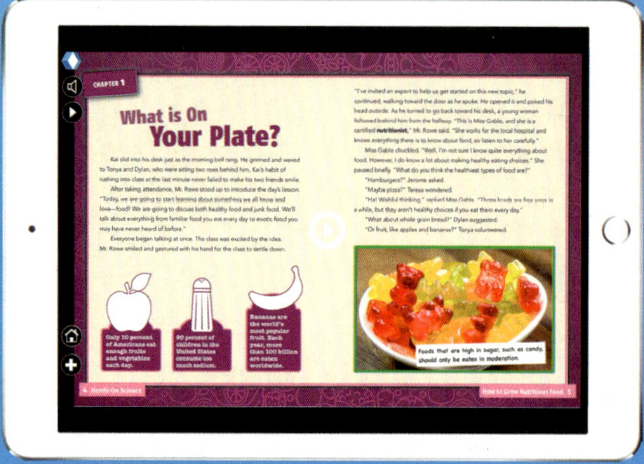

Lightbox is an all-inclusive digital solution for the teaching and learning of curriculum topics in an original, groundbreaking way. Lightbox is based on National Curriculum Standards.

STANDARD FEATURES OF LIGHTBOX

AUDIO High-quality narration using text-to-speech system

ACTIVITIES Printable PDFs that can be emailed and graded

SLIDESHOWS Pictorial overviews of key concepts

VIDEOS Embedded high-definition video clips

WEBLINKS Curated links to external, child-safe resources

TRANSPARENCIES Step-by-step layering of maps, diagrams, charts, and timelines

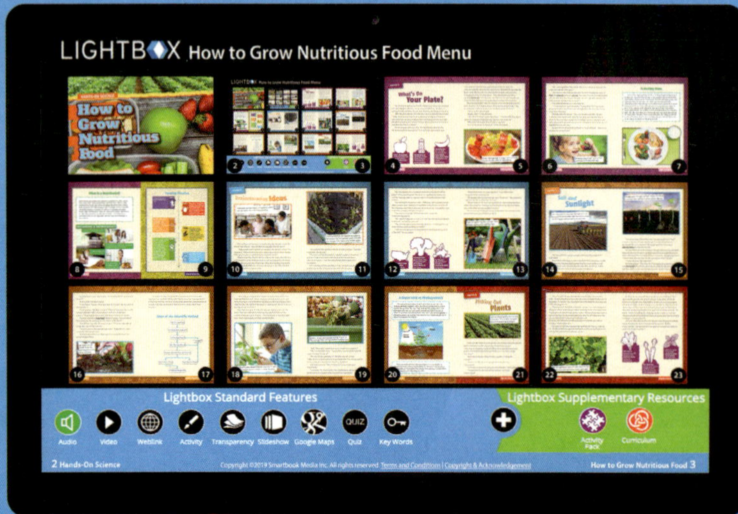

INTERACTIVE MAPS Interactive maps and aerial satellite imagery

QUIZZES Ten multiple choice questions that are automatically graded and emailed for teacher assessment

KEY WORDS Matching key concepts to their definitions

TABLE OF CONTENTS

CHAPTER 1

Waste In The Lunchroom

Kate and Andre began gathering their things as their lunch period ended. It was almost time for afternoon classes to start. First, though, they had to throw away their trash.

"Why are you throwing out your crusts?" Andre asked. "That's like tossing half of your sandwich in the garbage."

"I just don't like them," Kate replied. "Besides, you're throwing food away, too. You only ate part of that apple."

"I guess you're right," Andre said. "But I'm too full to eat any more."

Kate and Andre lined up to toss their trash in the cafeteria's big plastic bins. As they waited, they noticed that almost all the other kids were throwing food away, too. "Now that I'm thinking about it, it really does seem wasteful to throw out all of this food," Kate said.

"Hmm." Andre wrinkled his face in thought. "There has to be something else we can do with all these food scraps."

"Maybe we could think of a solution," Kate answered. "If we come up with a good plan, maybe the school will let us try it out!"

Just then, Ms. Michaels walked past carrying a tray of food. Ms. Michaels helped make and serve food in the school cafeteria. She always seemed to be in a good mood. The kids loved chatting with her at lunchtime. "What are you guys up to?" she asked Kate and Andre.

"We were just talking about the cafeteria's food scraps," Andre told her. "They must create a ton of waste. We want to cut down the amount of food we throw away."

"That's a great idea," Ms. Michaels replied. "I see just how much food gets tossed out every day. You wouldn't believe how quickly the trash cans fill up. We have to empty them after every lunch period!"

U.S. schools throw away about 0.5 pounds (0.23 kilograms) of food per student each week.

"Do you think the school would listen if we came up with a plan?" Kate asked.

"Of course!" Ms. Michaels answered. "And, if you don't mind, I have an idea. It might help put you on the right track for solving this problem."

"We don't mind at all," Andre said. "Tell us!"

"Well," Ms. Michaels began, "at home, my family and I don't throw our food waste in the trash. Instead, we put it in a **compost** pile. We have a small field where we grow a few **crops**. The compost makes great **fertilizer** to help our plants grow!"

"Food scraps can help your crops grow?" Kate asked, wrinkling her face in confusion.

"Well, not immediately," Ms. Michaels answered. "They need to **decompose** first. The material left behind after decomposition is full of the **nutrients** that plants need to grow." She paused for a moment to think. "Tell you what," she said. "Why don't you both come visit the farm this weekend. Then you can see for yourselves how it works."

"Wow," said Andre. "That sounds great!"

"Yeah!" Kate agreed. "I'll ask my mom if she can give us a ride."

Other materials that can be composted include coffee grounds, ashes, and sawdust.

The Compost Cycle

In a compost pile, life-forms called **decomposers** feed on food scraps and other waste. This process turns the waste into a material rich in substances that will help plants grow. Parts of those same plants might eventually end up back in the compost pile. They will help fertilize the next plants to grow. The natural world is one big, complex, never-ending cycle!

Compost Timeline

2300 BC

The Akkadians, in what is now Iraq, keep records on stone tablets. This includes one of the first known written references to composting.

160 BC

Roman General Cato the Elder writes *De Agri Cultura* (On Farming). This book is the oldest remaining Latin book, and contains descriptions of composting using worms.

1840 AD

German scientist Justus von Liebig finds that plants are able to obtain energy from different chemicals. This led to the use of more chemical fertilizers.

1905

Sir Albert Howard, an agronomist from Great Britain, begins to develop a way of creating better compost called the Indore Method.

1995

The Environmental Protection Agency (EPA) sees an increase in the amount of composting performed in the United States by more than 3 million tons (2.7 million metric tons) since 1990.

2017

New York City expands its curbside organic recycling service. By the end of 2018, all New Yorkers will be able to drop off waste to be composted.

CHAPTER 2

At the Farm

There are more than 2 million farms in the United States.

That Saturday, Kate's mom dropped Kate and Andre off at Ms. Michaels's house. She waved to them as she drove off down the country road back toward town.

"Wow," said Kate. "Your yard is huge, Ms. Michaels!"

Andre had already started walking toward the large field of plants growing nearby. "Are those green beans?" he asked. "They're my favorite!"

"We grow all kinds of vegetables here," Ms. Michaels answered. "There is some lettuce over there. Carrots are poking up over there. If you walk a little further, you'll spot the tomatoes and peppers."

"Everything looks so fresh and colorful," Kate observed as they walked through the field. "You could make a whole salad just from the things growing here!"

"Go ahead and pick a couple of those cherry tomatoes," Ms. Michaels said. "They look perfectly ripe."

Andre and Kate each picked a tiny tomato. They rubbed the tomatoes clean on their shirts and popped the fruits into their mouths. "Holy cow!" Andre said. "This is the best tomato I've ever tasted."

"You can thank the compost pile for that," Ms. Michaels replied. "It's a big part of why our plants grow so well."

"Andre and I did some reading online about composting," Kate said. "But I'm still not sure I understand how it works."

"Well," said Ms. Michaels, "come this way, and you can see how we do it here."

Kate and Andre followed as she led them toward a rectangular wooden bin off to the side of the field. She pulled a tarp off the top, and the kids peered inside. They saw a huge mound of dark material that looked almost like dirt. Mixed in was everything from apple cores and eggshells to grass and pieces of old newspaper.

"This is compost?" Andre asked. Ms. Michaels nodded. He stood up on his toes for a better view inside the bin. "It looks like a pile of trash and dirt."

Ms. Michaels laughed. "That's actually a pretty close guess."

"So how does it all work?" Kate asked. "You can just throw anything in there and it turns into dirt?"

"Not quite," Ms. Michaels replied. "Only certain kinds of materials are compostable. Also, you need to keep an eye on the pile. You might have to make adjustments from time to time."

"So what kinds of things can we put in a compost pile?" Kate asked.

"Hold on," Andre piped up as he pulled a notebook and pen from his backpack. "I've got an idea. Let's make a chart so we'll have an easier time remembering how this all works."

"Good thinking," said Ms. Michaels. She waited as Andre drew a T-shaped chart in his notebook. He labeled one side of the chart "Compostable" and the other side "Non-compostable."

"Okay," he said once the chart was completed. "Let's get started."

Ms. Michaels explained that everything in a compost pile must be **organic**. This means the materials need to come from **organisms**.

Each year, thousands of Christmas trees are composted.

"So, in other words, no plastic, metal, or glass," Kate said.

"Exactly," Ms. Michaels replied. "Those sorts of things won't decompose. Paper, pieces of wood, food scraps, and yard trimmings are all fine, though. Even hair, dryer lint, and old cotton rags can be composted." She added that certain organic materials were bad for composting. For example, meat and dairy products might cause the pile to smell bad as they decompose. They can also attract insects and other pests.

Andre wrote down the last few non-compostable items that Ms. Michaels had mentioned. "Got it," he said. "So now we know what kinds of materials we can use. How do we actually get the compost pile rolling?"

"And how do we know if it's working?" Kate asked. "How long does it take for scraps to turn into compost?"

"Those are all good questions," Ms. Michaels responded. "Maintaining a compost pile is pretty simple. The compost mostly takes care of itself. However, there are a couple of things you should watch out for." She explained that the best compost piles are made from a good mix of different materials. The pile will not work well if it is made entirely of grass clippings, for example. The materials also need to be broken into small pieces. "You can't let them clump together," Ms. Michaels said as she used a pitchfork to spread out a pile of wet leaves. The leaves had bunched up in one corner of the compost bin. She then began scooping up piles of compost and turning them over. "You also need to turn your compost every now and again. This means moving material from the bottom of the pile to cover the stuff on top."

"Why does that matter?" Andre asked. "It's all in the bin anyway."

"Turning the pile helps expose the compost to air," Ms. Michaels explained. "**Bacteria** and other life-forms living in the pile need air to do their job. They decompose all the materials in the pile, so we need to keep those life-forms healthy." She went on to say that the bacteria also need moisture. "If the pile is too dry, you might need to add a little water."

"This is all a lot to keep in mind," Andre said. He scribbled more notes next to his chart.

"You'll get the hang of it," Ms. Michaels promised. "Just let me know if you have any other questions as you work on your plan."

Compost should be turned once a week.

A Closer Look at Decomposers

There are many different types of decomposers. In a compost pile, bacteria are usually the most common ones. These tiny creatures feed on organic materials. They produce substances such as nitrogen and magnesium as waste. Luckily, plants use these substances to grow. The bacteria also produce heat as they work. As the compost pile grows hotter, new types of bacteria begin taking over.

Fungi are another common type of decomposer. These life-forms thrive in temperatures lower than the average compost pile. As a result, fungi are not as common as bacteria are in compost. However, they might appear once the pile is almost done decomposing and is beginning to cool down.

Finally, compost is often full of larger creatures such as worms and insects. They feed on bacteria and fungi as well as the organic material in the compost itself. As they move through the compost, they help mix it up. They also create passages that allow oxygen inside. This all helps speed up the decomposition process.

Bacteria

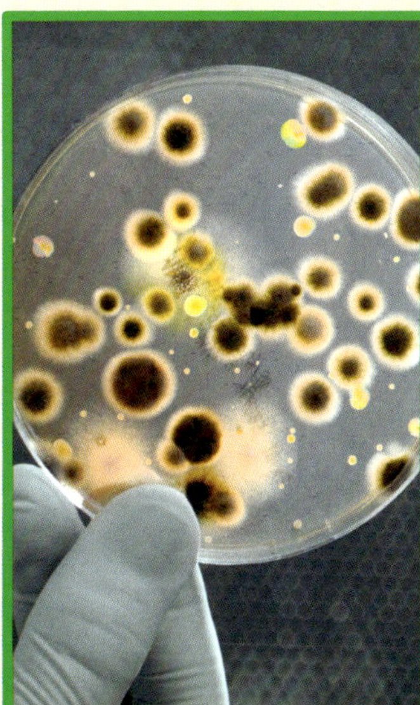

Fungi

mold

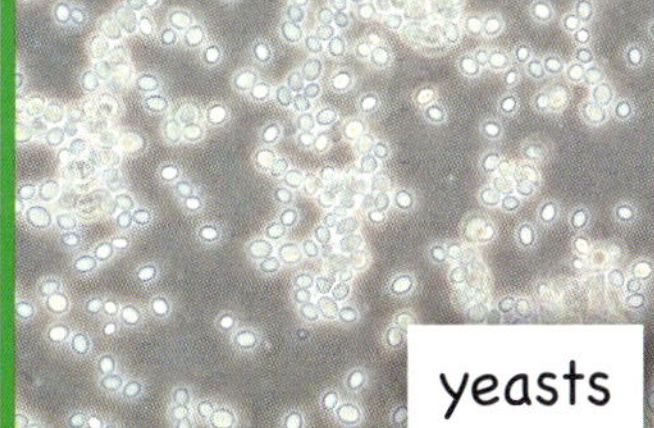

yeasts

Large Decomposers

earthworms

slugs

millipedes

CHAPTER 3

Putting the Plan In Motion

Many common cafeteria products, such as plastic plates, utensils, and packaging, cannot be composted.

The next day, Kate and Andre met at the library. They wanted to come up with a plan for their composting project. "Okay," Andre said. "We have all the information from Ms. Michaels. Now let's analyze it to see how composting might help with the trash problem at school."

Kate pointed at Andre's open notebook. "A lot of the things we throw away in the cafeteria are in the 'Compostable' section of our chart," she said.

"Yeah," Andre replied. "But there are also a lot of common trash items from the 'Non-compostable' side."

"In other words, we can't just dump the cafeteria trash bins into a compost pile," Kate added. "We'll need two separate cans."

"We'll also need to let everyone know what goes in each trash can," Andre pointed out.

"Maybe we could put up posters near the trash cans," Kate suggested.

"Good idea," said Andre. "We could also give a presentation during each lunch period for a day. Then, if anyone has questions, they can ask."

"Perfect," Kate answered. "Now we just have to figure out what we need to build the compost bin itself."

"The first thing we'll need is some space," Andre said. "Maybe we could build the bin in that grassy area outside the school's east entrance."

"That would be perfect," Kate said. "Not a lot of people use that entrance, so it won't be in the way. Also, it's close to the cafeteria. It would be easy to carry the compost material to the bin."

"We'll also need a few supplies," Andre added. "Building the bin requires wood and nails. We'll need a big pitchfork for turning the compost, too."

"Maybe Ms. Michaels could help us get those things," Kate said.

"Right!" said Andre. "Just a few more things to organize and we'll be good to go."

Kate nodded in agreement. The two friends began working on a document detailing their plan. They would use the document to present their idea to Mrs. Johnson, the school's principal.

Later that week, Andre and Kate met up with Ms. Michaels after school. The three of them had scheduled a meeting with Mrs. Johnson to explain their plan.

"I'm so nervous," Kate said as they walked toward the principal's office. "What if she says no?"

"I think she'll like the idea," Ms. Michaels replied. "You've got a great plan here, so don't worry!"

Mrs. Johnson greeted them with a smile as they walked into her office. "Hello there. Ms. Michaels tells me you have an idea for cutting down on the trash we throw away."

"We sure do," Andre replied.

Kate handed Mrs. Johnson the document about the project. "We want to create a compost pile," Kate said. "Setting it up is really easy, and it only requires a few supplies."

"That sounds good to me," Mrs. Johnson said. She read the list of items they would need to build the compost pile. "And Ms. Michaels is going to help you find these supplies?"

"Sure thing!" Ms. Michaels responded.

Starting with a small pilot program can help develop the steps used in a larger, school-wide composting program.

"Once the pile is up and running, it will be easy to maintain," Andre continued. "Kate and I can visit the pile every few days. We'll take measurements and make sure the material is decomposing properly."

"We can also turn the compost when it needs it," Kate added.

"And check to make sure it doesn't smell bad!" Andre piped in.

"It looks like you've put a lot of thought into this," Mrs. Johnson said. "Let's give it a try and see what happens. When do you want to get started?"

"Right away!" Kate and Andre said at almost exactly the same time.

The Right Stuff

Experts recommend that compost piles contain roughly equal amounts of "brown" and "green" materials. Another thing to consider is particle size. Alternating layers of larger chunks with tiny things helps improve airflow in the pile.

Types of Compost Materials

CHAPTER 4

The Perfect Balance

Compost bins can be made of wood or plastic.

A couple of days later, Kate and Andre spoke about composting during each of the school's lunch periods. By the end of the day, they had two huge cans of materials they could use to start their compost pile. After school, they met Ms. Michaels outside the school's east entrance. They helped her unload the supplies from her truck and started building a wooden composting box. Ms. Michaels had already measured the wood to make the box's sides about 5 feet (1.5 meters) long and 3 feet (0.9 m) tall.

After they finished building the box, they filled it with the compostable waste from the cafeteria. Finally, they emptied a bucket of soil from Ms. Michael's field onto the pile. They spread it into an even layer.

"This will help get things started," she said.

"All we have to do now is wait for it to start working," Kate said. She and Andre high-fived.

Just as they had promised, Kate and Andre checked on the pile after school every couple of days. Around a week after the compost pile was started, Ms. Michaels brought Kate and Andre a metal thermometer. It had a long needle.

"Measuring temperature is one of the most important parts of maintaining a good compost pile," she said. "We talked about temperature a little when you visited my farm. However, I don't think we discussed the details. Decomposers give off heat as they break down the materials in the pile."

"So the pile should warm up as it decomposes, right?" Andre asked.

"Exactly," Ms. Michaels replied.

"So temperature is how we know whether the compost pile is working," Kate said as she pulled out her phone. She did a quick search online. "It says here that a healthy compost pile should usually measure between 90 and 140 degrees Fahrenheit (32 and 60 degrees Celsius)."

"That's about right," Ms. Michaels responded. "Sometimes it might get even hotter than that. But if you ever notice the temperature dropping, it's time to turn the compost or add more material."

"Got it," Andre said. He added the information to his notebook.

About a week later, Kate and Andre noticed that the pile had developed a bad smell. "Yuck," Kate said. "What should we do?"

Andre searched online for information about odors in compost piles. "It looks like this can happen if the pile has too much moisture."

"But Ms. Michaels told us that decomposers work best in wet material," Kate said.

"The compost should be moist but not too moist," Andre said. "And a lot of the things we put in here from the cafeteria are pieces of fruits and vegetables. Those things have a lot of water in them. Also, it just rained yesterday."

"Based on that information, we might fix the smell by adding more dry materials," Kate concluded.

"Hey, that's right," Andre said, pointing at the chart in his notebook. "Paper is compostable. Why don't we go inside? Maybe we can take some from the classroom recycling cans."

"Perfect," said Kate. "But don't forget, we need to shred it before we add it to the pile. Smaller pieces will help it decompose faster."

About 20 to 30 percent of garbage thrown away by people in the United States is material that can be composted.

5.1%

About 5.1 percent of food in the United States was composted in 2014.

One inch (2 centimeters) of compost is enough to help start a new garden.

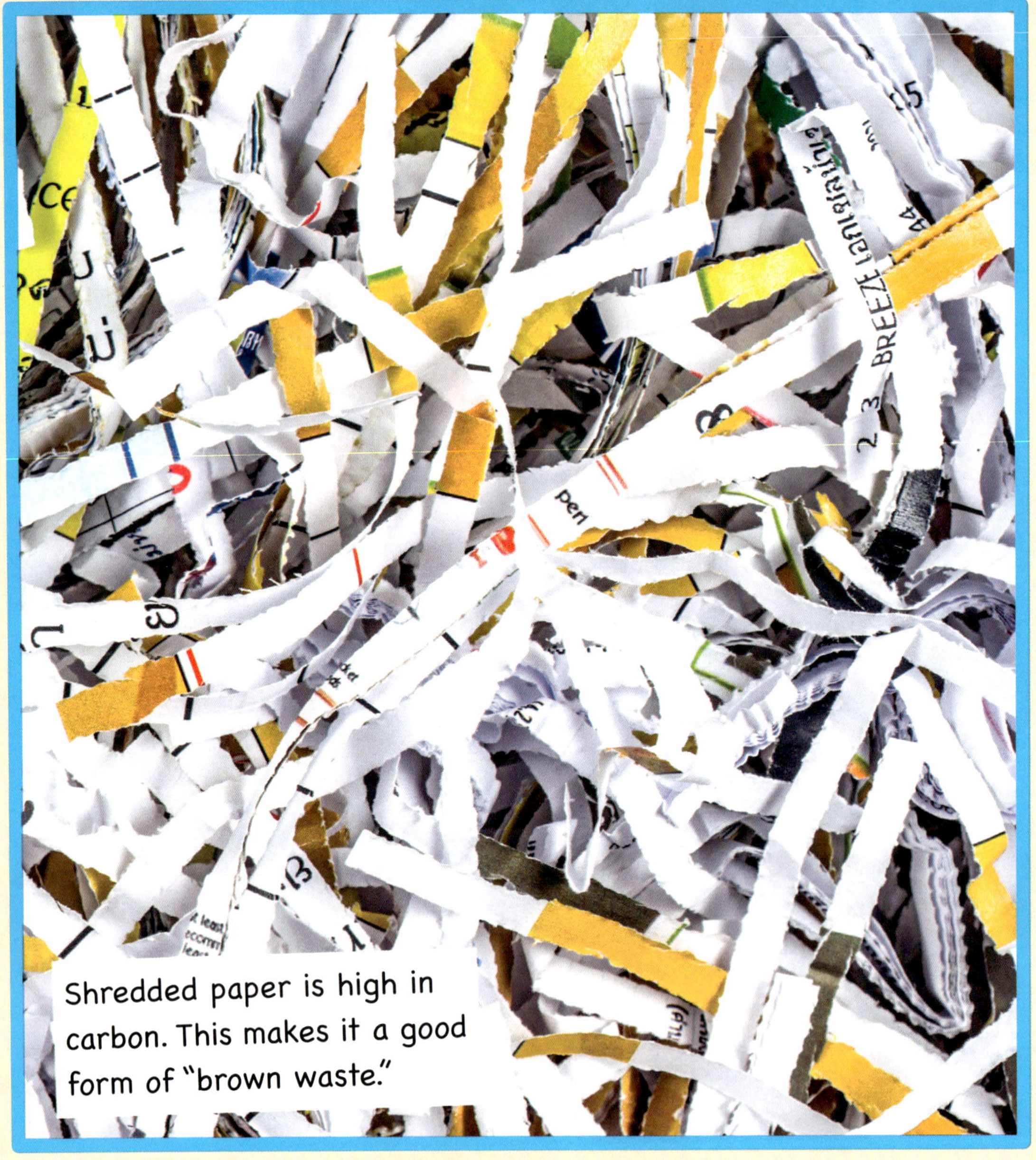

Shredded paper is high in carbon. This makes it a good form of "brown waste."

"Now that I'm thinking about it, Ms. Michaels used a tarp to cover the compost pile at her house," Andre continued. "If we cover our pile, we can keep the rain from throwing the mix off balance."

"Good thinking," said Kate. "I'll go ask around for some dry paper while you ask Ms. Michaels about the tarp."

CHAPTER 5

Spreading the Word

Industrial compost is screened before being packaged to make sure no metal or plastic remains.

Kate and Andre added paper to the mix and covered the box with a tarp. Within a few days, the pile stopped smelling bad. Ms. Michaels showed Kate and Andre how to measure the compost's moisture levels. Together, they weighed a sample from the pile, dried it in an oven, and then weighed it again. The difference in weight showed how much moisture was in the pile. Kate and Andre decided to do this every two weeks to make sure the pile would not smell bad again. They also kept a close eye on the temperature and turned the pile regularly.

One sunny afternoon several months later, Mrs. Johnson joined Kate and Andre outside. She wanted a closer look at the pile. Andre showed her a scoop of the rich, black dirt from the bottom of the pile.

"I'm really impressed," Mrs. Johnson said. "Would you mind if I took some of this home to spread in my flower garden?"

"That would be great," Kate said.

"We've actually been wondering what to do with all of this compost now that it's done decomposing," Andre added.

The heat produced during composting can help kill any harmful germs in the material.

"Why don't we share it with people in the community?" Mrs. Johnson suggested. "I could organize an event for local gardeners to come and collect the compost. You could even give a presentation about the project, if you're interested."

"That sounds fun," Kate said.

"Yeah," said Andre. "Maybe we can even convince some people to start compost piles of their own."

The big event was scheduled for a Saturday afternoon a couple of weeks later. Students, parents, teachers, and other local people turned up. Everyone wanted to hear what Kate and Andre had to say.

"That's a lot of people!" Kate said as they prepared to start the presentation.

"Don't worry," Ms. Michaels told her. "You're going to do great!"

"I sure hope so," Andre responded.

Minutes later, the two friends stepped out in front of the applauding crowd as Mrs. Johnson introduced them. The audience listened carefully as Kate and Andre explained how they had decided to start composting. Andre told them about the trip to Ms. Michaels's farm. Kate explained how they used what they learned to create a plan for the school compost pile. They also discussed how composting worked and told the crowd about solving their pile's odor problem. Finally, they asked if anyone had any questions.

"Can you help me start a compost pile of my own?" asked Mr. Webster, their math teacher.

"Me too!" Andre's mom added. The crowd laughed.

"We can definitely give you all of the information you need," Kate replied with a smile.

Soil with compost needs less water than soil without any.

"I've got a question for you," said Mrs. D'Angelo. She was an older woman who lived across the street from the school. "Now that you have all this great compost, have you thought about starting a school garden?"

"Wow," said Andre. "That's a fantastic idea!"

Kate nodded in agreement. "I guess it's time for us to start gathering information and planning our next project," she said. She and Andre grinned at each other as the crowd began applauding.

Composting in the United States

For much of the history of the United States, people have found ways to reuse waste. People have been composting in the country for hundreds of years. Today, many private companies, city initiatives, and local groups take part in composting around the country. How is food waste recycled near you?

Quiz

1. What are most compost bins made of?

2. What kind of decomposer is yeast?

3. What percent of food sold in the United States is thrown away without being eaten?

4. Which president had one of the first U.S. buildings made for composting in his estate?

5. What happens to industrial compost before it is packaged?

6. Can pet hair be composted?

7. How often should compost be turned?

8. What can help kill harmful germs in compost material?

9. Should compost contain more "brown" or "green" material?

10. When did Sir Albert Howard develop the Indore Method?

Answers: 1. Wood or plastic 2. A fungus 3. Between 4 and 10 4. George Washington 5. It is screened for plastic or metal 6. Yes 7. Once a week 8. The heat produced during composting 9. It should have equal amounts of both 10. 1905

Key Words

bacteria: tiny, single-celled living things that are found everywhere and may be useful or harmful

compost: a mixture of organic material that is added to soil to make it more productive

crops: plants grown for food for people or animals

decompose: to rot or decay

decomposers: organisms that help break down organic matter by consuming it

fertilizer: an organic or man-made substance used to make the soil richer so that plants grow better

fungi: plantlike organisms that have no leaves, flowers, roots, or chlorophyll and grow on other plants or decaying matter

nutrients: substances needed for plants and animals to be healthy

organic: from or produced by living things

organisms: living things, such as plants or animals

Index

LIGHTBOX

SUPPLEMENTARY RESOURCES

Click on the plus icon ⊕ found in the bottom left corner of each spread to open additional teacher resources.

- Download and print the book's quizzes and activities
- Access curriculum correlations
- Explore additional web applications that enhance the Lightbox experience

LIGHTBOX DIGITAL TITLES

Packed full of integrated media

VIDEOS

INTERACTIVE MAPS

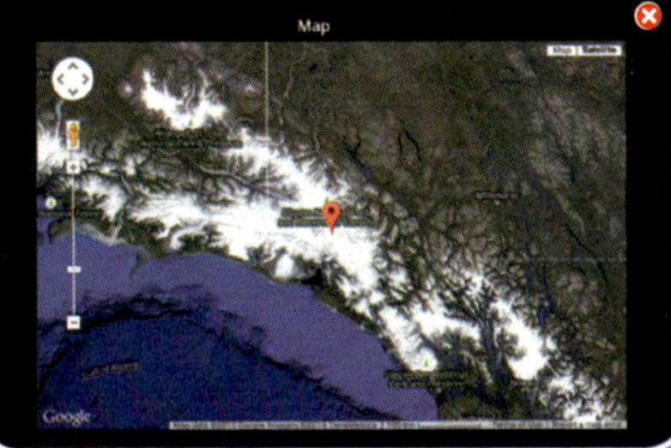

WEBLINKS

SLIDESHOWS

QUIZZES

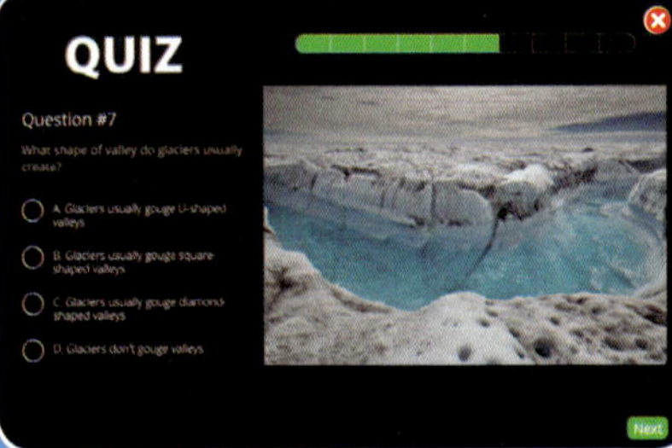

OPTIMIZED FOR

- ✓ TABLETS
- ✓ WHITEBOARDS
- ✓ COMPUTERS
- ✓ AND MUCH MORE!

Published by Smartbook Media Inc.
350 5th Avenue, 59th Floor
New York, NY 10118
Website: www.openlightbox.com

Project Coordinator John Willis
Designer Sushant Deshpande

Library of Congress Cataloging-in-Publication Data
Names: Gregory, Josh, author | Willis, John, author.
Title: How to compost at school / Josh Gregory and John Willis.
Description: [2018 edition]. | New York, NY : Smartbook Media Inc., [2018] |
Series: Hands-On Science | Includes index.
Identifiers: LCCN 2017056336 (print) | LCCN 2017054941 (ebook) | ISBN 9781510537248 (hard cover : alk. paper) | ISBN 9781510537255 (Multi-User eBook)
Subjects: LCSH: Compost--Juvenile literature. | Fertilizers--Juvenile literature. | Gardening--Juvenile literature. | School lunchrooms, cafeterias, etc.--Management--Juvenile literature.
Classification: LCC S661 .G74 2018 (ebook) | LCC S661 (print) | DDC 631.8/75--dc23
LC record available at https://lccn.loc.gov/2017056336

052018
110117
Printed in Brainerd, Minnesota, United States
1 2 3 4 5 6 7 8 9 0 22 21 20 19 18

Photo Credits
The publisher acknowledges Getty Images, iStock, Shutterstock, and Alamy as its primary image suppliers for this title.